CLAR-INNSE

CONTENTS

Text by John Love (SNH)

Boreray and its Stacs from North Uist

Bho thòiseachadh luaisgeach gharg

From **violent** beginnings

AN EVOLVING STORY SGEULACHD AIR A TOIRT GU BITH

St Kilda erupted on to the scene some
50 to 60 million years ago when the
Atlantic Ocean began to split apart.
This mighty tear in the Earth's crust
separated the ancient rocks of Greenland
from similar rocks in the Hebrides.
A period of violent activity followed,
with St Kilda being one in a series of
volcanoes scattered from Northern
Ireland up through the Inner Hebrides.

Conachair

The ash deposits and lava flows produced by the St Kilda volcano have long since been worn away. Only the hard resistant rocks remain, called gabbros and granites, from deep within its heart. Recent offshore surveys have revealed the outline of St Kilda's original caldera on the sea bed, indicating how the scattered, craggy islands we see today once linked up along its edge. The whole structure collapsed inwards, leaving a circular platform 60m below the present sea surface. Beyond this the sea bed drops to some 140m deep.

The oldest rocks exposed on St Kilda today are the gabbros on the Cambir and Dùn. These are coarse, granular and rich in iron, making them better able to stand up to the elements. Molten lava then intruded into any lines of weakness, cooling quickly into a fine-grained complex of dykes that appears as black streaks on cliff faces. The islands of Soay, Boreray, Levenish and parts of the main island of Hirta are themselves made up of a crushed mix of these gabbros and lavas.

A few million years later, fresh magma cooled more slowly to produce medium to fine-grained granite, rich in silica. This is a distinctive cream, grey or pink colour, with occasional larger pink or white crystals of minerals such as felspar and quartz. The centre of Hirta is a complex mix of dark gabbro fragments amongst this granite magma.

The granite of Conachair represents the last major volcanic event in St Kilda's history, dating back about 55 million years and making up much of the northeast part of Hirta, including Oiseval. Granite is less resistant to erosion than gabbro, so the hills of eastern Hirta are smooth and rounded in appearance, in contrast to its ragged north and west coast. All volcanic activity finally finished about 35 million years ago, with the injection of a new and extensive suite of dykes and sills of black, fine-grained lava, especially visible in the high sea cliffs north of Conachair.

A' cumadh sealladh na tìre

Shaping the **landscape**

TEMPERED BY THE OCEAN   AIR A RIAGHLADH LEIS AN FHAIRGE

For millions of years, St Kilda has withstood all that the elements and seas could throw at it. Even today, variations in the hardness and make-up of different rock types are exploited at different rates by the severe Atlantic storms. These continue to sculpt its 35 km coastline into dramatic ramparts of wonderful variety and form. At just over 400m, the sheer rock face of Conachair forms the highest sea cliff in the British Isles, while the whole cluster of islands boasts a superb range of sea caves, arches, geos, tunnels, blowholes and stacks. Indeed, at 191m, Stac an Armin, off the northern tip of Boreray, is the highest sea stack in Britain.

While wind and wave have shaped the coast, the present landscape inland owes a great deal to the effects of the last Ice Age. There is some debate as to whether ice sheets from the mainland ever reached St Kilda, but the glen behind Village Bay in Hirta certainly spawned its own little glacier about 18,000 years ago. Both major streams (in Glen Bay and in Village Bay) are misfits, in that their U-shaped valleys were made bigger by ice action rather than water. Weathered debris from the slopes above was deposited as boulder clay or till on the floor of the glen.

Most of the higher slopes are covered by frost shattered rocks, with the finest scree slopes occurring around Village Bay, below Conachair and below Mullach Sgar. Carn Mòr is an extreme example, where boulders span up to seven metres across. Similar block fields are strewn over Soay, Boreray and even – albeit on a much reduced scale – on the summit of Stac an Armin. If any of St Kilda remained free from ice, it would have been exposed to extreme Arctic conditions and we can be fairly confident that little or no life survived.

The last Ice Age would have effectively wiped the slate clean, ready for a completely new wave of colonists.

▲ Carn Mòr boulder field on Hirta

St Kilda's environment nowadays is tempered by the ocean, with mild winters and cool summers. The archipelago's daily range of temperatures (6°C in summer and 3° in winter) is the narrowest anywhere in Britain, apart from the Scillies. Frost and snow are rare, as are calm days. The cool, wet climate of St Kilda not only reduces biological activity but also increases the flushing of nutrients. Together these result in poor, acid, peaty soils. The islands are too steep for a lot of peat to form, although some occurs even on the summit of Hirta. The islanders used to cut moorland turf as fuel near the village; misguidedly, since this exposed the soils to erosion. Manure from seabirds and sheep adds nitrogen, phosphate and calcium to St Kilda's soils, while salt spray contributes magnesium, sodium and potassium.

Probably the windiest place in Britain

This is probably the windiest place in Britain. St Kilda experiences gales on 75 days of the year - that is twice as much as Benbecula, only 45 km to the east. Driven by fierce winds, winter storms throw huge boulders up on the beach at Village Bay, and can cause major structural damage to buildings, especially on the summit of Mullach Mòr. At about 1200mm, the annual rainfall is barely twice that of Edinburgh, but it is evenly spread through the year, with high humidity.

What is St Kilda?

The St Kilda archipelago, 64 kilometres west of the Outer Hebrides, comprises four main islands – Hirta, Dùn, Soay and Boreray – and their surrounding rock stacks, notably Levenish, Stac Lee and Stac an Armin. There never was a saint called 'Kilda' and the name has long been thought to have been a printing error on early maps. However, a more convincing explanation for its origin comes from the Gaelic-speaking islanders' peculiar habit of pronouncing 'r' like an 'l'. Thus they spoke the name of the main island – Hirte or Hiort – like 'Hilte' or 'Hilt'.

Toiseach beatha nan lus

Plant life makes landfall

TOUGH ON THE EDGE   CRUADAL AIR AN IOMALL

The severity and extent of recent glaciations means that we only need to consider the colonisation of St Kilda since the last ice melted and the climate became bearable for life to return. It is extremely unlikely that St Kilda was ever connected to the Hebrides by a land bridge, so organisms can reach it in only three ways - by air, by sea or as a passenger with something else. The islands are 64 km from the next nearest land, against the prevailing southwesterly winds and currents, so they present a small target for potential colonists. This isolation and small size means St Kilda's modern flora and fauna is relatively impoverished.

▲   Roseroot

Boreray shrouded in mist ▶

Plants that produce tiny airborne spores – such as mosses, lichens, fungi and ferns – are the most likely pioneers. St Kilda is surprisingly well endowed in some of these departments. Nearly 200 species of larger fungi have been recorded on St Kilda, together with 56 species of liverworts, 104 mosses and 194 lichens.

Many higher plants, such as grasses, produce light airborne seeds while others, such as the daisy/dandelion family (Compositae), have developed parachute mechanisms to help them disperse. For some unknown reason though, composites are poorly represented on St Kilda. Other plant seeds, especially coastal ones, can float using air spaces to make their

seeds more buoyant. Many are also well able to withstand being immersed in salt water.

Birds provide transport for certain plants and animals. Some seeds are sticky or have hooks, specially to hitch a lift on birds, while others can still grow after passing through the bird's gut. Thus some pioneering

◀ Lichen heath on the summit of Hirta looking down to Village Bay and Dùn

Lousewort ▶

plants might be found growing out of bird droppings or on carcasses washed up on a beach.

Many plants with poor dispersal abilities are entirely absent from offshore islands. Even if some species do manage to complete the journey they might find conditions unsuitable for survival. St Kilda only has 184 species of flowering plants, grasses and ferns, compared with some 700 on the Outer Hebrides. The archipelago has no proper trees or shrubs. In addition, there are few representatives of some plant families, such as Labiates and Composites.

With limited competitors, those that do thrive can often expand into habitats that would otherwise be occupied by plants that are absent. So on St Kilda you find meadow buttercups, for example, living in drier places typical of bulbous buttercups, as well as in wet places typical of creeping buttercups, neither of which have managed to establish.

Tough on the edge

Nowhere on St Kilda escapes the

▲　Thrift on Dùn

▲　Scurvygrass

influence of the salt-laden winds. On the windiest cliffs and shores only the most salt-tolerant plants can survive. These include plants like sea plantain, sea pink, sea campion and fescue grass. Hirta, Boreray and Soay are heavily grazed by sheep in summer, but winter winds and rain tend to prevent much dung enrichment. The most extreme – rank sorrel, scurvy grass and mayweed – are found only amongst the bird colonies on the less exposed, ungrazed island of Dùn.

Lichens thrive on large, guano-spattered boulders in seabird colonies like those on Dùn and Carn Mòr (with up to 25 species on a single, well-manured boulder). The rare *Lecanora straminea* has even colonised the aluminium body of the crashed Wellington bomber on Soay! Furthermore, salt tolerant mosses and liverworts are remarkably lush on St Kilda, even at the summit of Conachair. Ferns do well in sheltered cliff crevices, thriving in the humid atmosphere.

Between the 30 and 40 metre contours, the slopes of Hirta are especially rich in lichens. Here they form a close-cropped pasture with up to 12 species per square metre.

Lower down, around Village Bay, the islanders grew crops using an organic fertiliser of domestic and animal waste, offal, bird carcases and old thatch. This practice declined and had stopped altogether by 1930, but the high nutrient status of this soil still supports no fewer than nine kinds of earthworm.

The Soay sheep also have a great liking for these rich and abandoned grasslands. This grassland is tussocky, with bent grass and Yorkshire fog, while its close-cropped gaps are dominated by clover, creeping bent grass, meadow grass, fescue and sweet vernal grass, along with mosses and liverworts.

A more extreme grass community, called 'lair flora', flourishes behind walls and around the entrance of cleits, wherever sheep persistently

▲ Dark and tan Soay sheep amongst the cleits of Hirta

seek shelter and leave copious dung and urine. A dense and vigorous growth of Yorkshire fog and meadow grass results, along with the herbs mouse-ear, celandine and clover.

Damp, marshy areas support poor quality grasses and a variety of sphagnums and other mosses, as well as asphodel, sundew, sedges and rushes. Between the summits of Mullach Mòr and Conachair is a mix of peat hags and cottongrass where great skuas nest. Woodrush thrives on or near the drier summits, while the most windswept tops contain several interesting species including

St Kilda's only 'tree', the dwarf willow *Salix herbacea*, which is only a few centimetres high.

The main vegetation on the smaller island of Boreray is similar to the rich grasslands of Village Bay. However, it supports fewer species, perhaps because of its less varied landscape.

Although sheep also graze on Soay, the grasses there have less heather and crowberry than equivalent communities on Hirta. Its south-eastern slope in particular is much influenced by burrowing puffins, producing a fringe of plantains near the sea.

Boom or bust?

The numbers of Soay sheep on Hirta have varied from 600 to 2000 since 1957 and concerns are always expressed in peak years about the impact upon the vegetation. Grazing is intense during February and March of crash years when large numbers of sheep die. However, recent research has shown that the vegetation is very resilient and recovers quickly during the summer to be as good if not better than before. Although some plant species only occur on cliff sites that sheep cannot reach, some of the rarest flowers on Hirta, such as field gentian and purple saxifrage, thrive on the heavily grazed pastures. Where is no grazing at all – such as on Dùn, and many of the cleit roofs – species richness is poor compared with Hirta. So the sheep do not seem to have a harmful effect on the vegetation, nor are they eating themselves out of house and home.

Beathaichean agus biastagan a' ruighinn

Insects and other **animals** touch down

ISLAND PIONEERS   TÙSAIREAN NAN EILEAN

Animals have the same options as plants for crossing an ocean barrier – by sea, by air or as stowaways. But, just like plants, not all creatures are equipped to try, fewer will make it and some that do may fail to establish. Larger islands present a bigger target so they gather in more pioneers and are likely to offer a better variety of opportunities. Thus they can sustain a greater variety of species. However, there will be a limit to the resources they offer so, in time, new colonists may find it difficult to fit in. When a new arrival is particularly well adapted to the conditions, it may well outcompete some of the original inhabitants. Extinction is therefore a constant risk, especially when the population size on small islands is so limited. These are the fundamental principles of biogeography – the theory of how species reach, survive or perish on islands.

The storm beach, Village Bay, with Dùn behind ▶

Not many land animals will have managed to reach St Kilda by swimming or on rafts of vegetation. It is, after all, a long way out against the prevailing winds and currents and there are hardly any suitable beaches as landfalls. Perhaps some bark-living or wood-boring invertebrates arrived on driftwood along with the islands' modest collection of tiny soil creatures such as mites, collembolans (five species) and silverfish.

Beetles appear to be particularly intrepid, since there are 140 or so species recorded on St Kilda, including a small rare and endangered weevil (Ceutorhynchus insularis) restricted to scurvy grass on Dùn. Otherwise, it is only known from one of the Westmann Islands off Iceland. On the other hand, many other beetles one might expect to find are missing.

Similarly, St Kilda is lacking in other groups that you would think could easily fly there. Mayflies, dragonflies, stoneflies and lacewings never succeeded, but it is perhaps less surprising that there should be no grasshoppers. Only one species of scorpion fly has been recorded (though this old record is suspect) and one earwig, but there are ten types of caddisflies and about a score of bug species.

Only three of the seven lice are at all common, and two of them are wingless, with one species normally found in tree bark on the mainland. (On such windswept islands, insects can find it an acute disadvantage having wings, and in spending too much time flying around). A few lice are parasites on sheep and birds – and would originally have been stowaways on them while one tick Ixodes uriae is common in seabird nests. Nine species of flea have been found, seven in wren nests and two on mice.

Pollinators

By far the most successful insect colonists have been the flies (Diptera), with nearly 200 species recorded. Since there are no bees (Hymenoptera) and few butterflies and moths (Lepidoptera), flies may well be important in pollinating flowers.

Although there are at least 367 butterfly and moth species in the Outer Hebrides (which in itself is only about 14% of the British list), fewer than a hundred have made it out to St Kilda. (Only seven of these are butterflies.) Robust and widespread species that often migrate over long distances feature prominently on Hirta's list, such as the silver Y moth, red admiral and painted lady butterflies. Antler and dark arches are the most common moths, seen every summer, while there is one curious record of the rare least carpet moth *Idaea vulpinaria*, which normally lives in the south of England.

There have been no gastropods recorded in St Kilda, only three centipedes/millipedes, and only one ant. Over 60 species of spider have been collected, but two thirds of them belong to the family Linyphiidae or 'money spiders', which are accomplished balloonists. Their young spin threads of gossamer to aid dispersal by wind and thus have a unique capacity for reaching offshore islands.

On the other hand, only six kinds of harvestmen have been found in St Kilda. Harvestmen are at a disadvantage because they lack the waterproof protective coat of spiders. However, one widespread British species *Mitopus morio* reaches astonishing numbers at the damp, misty summit of Conachair, where the lush woodrush offers shelter from the drying winds. Here it lives alongside one spider *Pirata piraticus* whose thin, less effective waterproof coat confines it to damp marshy environments.

Silver Y moth ▶

Eòin-mhara
Seabirds

FIRST FOOTERS   NA CIAD CHEUMANNAN

It is highly likely that birds were the first creatures to set foot on the island after the Ice Age ended 10-15,000 years ago. Since meat-eating mammals usually fail to reach offshore islands without human help, these outposts offer secure breeding sites for seabirds that live in colonies. St Kilda's widespread rocky cliffs offer safe ledges suitable for breeding gannets and fulmars, while broader shelves are preferred by guillemots and razorbills. Kittiwakes can use the steepest faces by building a nest of mud, seaweed and guano against the rock, needing only the smallest outcrops as a foundation. Shags prefer boulder fields and scree slopes, often near the foot of cliffs, where a few black guillemots may also nest.

Razorbill

Gannet

Kittiwake

Fulmar

From Rio to Hirta . . . the aerial pirate

The 'bonxie' or great skua is a relative newcomer to St Kilda, only starting to breed there in the mid 1960s. There are now over 200 pairs on the archipelago. The bonxie is a far travelled migrant; some even journeying as far afield as Brazil. The name bonxie originates from the Shetland Isles, where it is used to describe a robust, aggressive individual. Never was a name more apt than for this 'pirate' of the skies, which harries other seabirds until they disgorge their hard-won fish.

The oceanic plant communities on St Kilda's less steep slopes support small colonies of gulls who rip up plants in courtship and use them to build their nest mounds. Thick soil allows puffins and shearwaters to burrow. Leach's storm petrels also like to dig nest holes but European storm petrels prefer cracks in the rock, such as the Carn Mòr boulder field, as well as walls and dry-stone structures.

St Kilda is one of the largest and most important seabird stations in the North Atlantic, supporting some 330,000 breeding pairs of 17 species. This must represent about a million birds at the height of the season. Five of these are numerous enough to be important in a British context, especially the northern gannet and puffin (30% and 25% of the UK populations respectively, although Iceland and Norway have more).

With 13% of the British population of northern fulmars, St Kilda has the oldest and largest colony in the country. New techniques to estimate the numbers of burrow-nesting seabirds have revealed that most of the Leach's storm petrels nesting in the eastern Atlantic are to be found in St Kilda, although still not as many as in North America. There are a lot fewer European storm petrels than were expected, but the numbers are still significant.

▲ Razorbills

The islands lie close to prime fishing grounds. In the daytime, Manx shearwaters mostly fly far westwards out to the edge of the Continental shelf. Here they plunge dive, to modest depths, hunting for a variety of small fish, cephalopods (such as squid) and crustaceans. Small petrels join them, but feed by pattering along the surface, taking tiny crustaceans and fish, probably mostly at night. Kittiwakes are daytime feeders, seeking shoals of sand eels near the surface.

Shags and black guillemots dive to catch small fish close to St Kilda, while guillemots and razorbills fly 30 km or more, towards the Hebrides. Similar to penguins, these auks are consummate divers and can reach depths of 180m to pursue sandeels, herring and sprats. Puffins also take sandeels but do not dive so deep, while gannets look for larger fish such as mackerel and herring. Gannet flocks indulge in dramatic plunge-dives, at speeds of up to 100 kph. They hit the water, with wings folded behind, like a snow-white javelin and achieve depths of about 15m.

▲ Puffins

Fulmars and gulls often follow fishing boats for scraps. This may have been the reason for their increase in numbers throughout Britain early last century. Nowadays, they have to rely on more natural food sources. Interestingly, St Kilda was the only breeding location for fulmars in the whole of Britain and Ireland until 1878, whereas they are now found nesting around the entire coastline. It is open to question whether St Kilda provided the source of birds for this dramatic spread. Breeding numbers on the archipelago have remained relatively stable, so the increase may have come from Iceland or farther north.

Finally, two other seabirds are relative newcomers to St Kilda's shores. The great skua first bred on Hirta in 1963, increasing by up to 20% per annum to peak at 233 pairs in 1997. Currently, there are 180 to 200 pairs, with a few also on Soay, Boreray and Dùn. One pair of Arctic skuas fledged two young on Hirta in 2000. Skuas harry other seabirds in the air to rob them of their catch, as they return to the colony. Arctic skuas perform agile and spectacular chases on kittiwakes, terns and gulls, while great skuas are big enough to take on gannets. They are also quite aggressive when dive-bombing humans who stray too near their nest.

The many books that have been written about the archipelago's unique human culture describe well how the St Kildans exploited seabirds. This seems to have been a sustainable activity and was certainly a vital one in the survival of the islanders.

The great auk

Only one species - the great auk - is known to have become extinct throughout its range as a result of human activity. St Kildans caught one in 1821, and then another on Stac an Armin around 1840, which proved the last British example. The great auk officially became extinct when the very last known pair was killed in Iceland in 1844.

Eòin-tìr

Land birds

RELUCTANT SEAFARERS   MARAICHEAN AINDEÒNACH

▲ Peregrine falcon feeding chicks

Almost any bird that flies could reach St Kilda, especially if it is helped by strong winds. Over a hundred species turn up in any year and 228 species have so far been recorded on the island, some rarely or only once. Since the first checklist was compiled in 1978, fifty new species have been added to it, about two a year on average.

Oystercatcher ▶

As far as we know, only 34 have ever bred on the islands. Some, like the peregrine and white-tailed sea eagle, probably nested regularly, others perhaps only occasionally. A few – such as the corn bunting, twite and corncrake – might have given up when people abandoned growing crops and left in 1930.

The pairs of oystercatchers have halved in recent years to about 25 but snipe have become more plentiful, with about 100 pairs in good seasons. About 50 pairs of eiders breed around the shore.

Only seven other 'land birds' now nest annually, the lowest since records began. There are some 300 pairs of starlings, 100 pairs of rock pipits, 30-60 pairs of wheatears and 20 pairs of meadow pipits. Several pairs of hooded crows and ravens seem to be resident too, although their nests are hard to find amongst the huge cliffs.

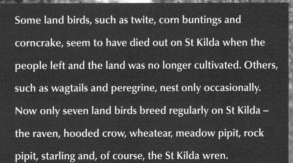

Some land birds, such as twite, corn buntings and corncrake, seem to have died out on St Kilda when the people left and the land was no longer cultivated. Others, such as wagtails and peregrine, nest only occasionally. Now only seven land birds breed regularly on St Kilda – the raven, hooded crow, wheatear, meadow pipit, rock pipit, starling and, of course, the St Kilda wren.

St Kilda wren

Surprising though it may seem, even the tiny wren reached St Kilda by flying. Populations have established in many other offshore islands in the North Atlantic (notably Fair Isle in Shetland), and have similarly become quite distinctive in appearance and habits. They all share adaptations enabling them to withstand the harsh, exposed conditions. The St Kilda wren is a recognised subspecies and is somewhat larger than the mainland wren. It has a thicker and stronger bill, along with a paler plumage more distinctly marked with bars.

At first, the St Kilda wren attracted quite a bit of attention from naturalists, museums and collectors, giving the human inhabitants of St Kilda a supplement to their meagre income by selling skins and eggs. Parliament therefore passed a special Act in 1904, which also protected the rare Leach's storm petrel. Wren numbers may indeed have dropped around the Village in Hirta but they were never in much danger, as the bird remained common on the steep and dangerous cliffs. Numbers probably total around 230 pairs – over 100 of them on Hirta, about 50 each on Boreray and Soay, another 25 or so on Dùn, and even 2-3 pairs near the summit of Stac an Armin.

▲ St Kilda wren

Wrens and puffins . . . an unlikely partnership

The wren's distribution is closely linked to the puffin and the highest densities are on Dùn and at Carn Mòr on Hirta. Dead fish and seabird carcases all support an abundance of carrion-eating insects upon which the wrens feed.

One of many wrens . . . but special nevertheless!

There are 79 species of wren in the world, and many more subspecies have been described. Several of the islands around Britain have their own distinct races, notably Shetland, Fair Isle and St Kilda. The St Kilda wren *Troglodytes troglodytes hirtensis* differs from its mainland 'cousin' by being somewhat larger while its plumage is paler and more distinctly marked. It seems to make a cruder nest too, and its eggs are slightly larger. The Latin name *Troglodytes* means 'cave dweller', and the St Kilda birds in particular spend most of their time sheltering amongst rocks on the cliffs.

Snipe on nest ▶

Luchainn Hiort

St Kilda **mice**

A STOWAWAY FAILS   CRÌOCH LUCHAINN NAM BÀTA

The wren is only one of three examples where St Kilda's challenging environment has used limited genetic material from a few original founders to mould unique and distinctive races. The other two are both mice, which arrived as stowaways with early human settlers, at most only a few thousand years ago. The house mouse's unusual features were first noted in 1874. But by 1906 it was accepted as merely a robust and pale form of the common house mouse *Mus musculus* on the mainland.

St Kilda house mouse

Male house mice could reach 105mm in length, with the tail as long again, and the largest individuals reached 32g in weight. House mice swarmed in all the houses and occurred in walls and cleits within the cultivated area. Sadly, they died out soon after humans left in 1930, perhaps killed by the few abandoned cats which themselves soon disappeared (leaving St Kilda, mercifully, free from land carnivores).

In 1905 house mice were widespread in the numerous walls and buildings. By supplying the local lads with traps, the naturalist and museum collector James Waterson procured as many mice as he wanted. He did note that they were omnivorous and very prolific, with 6 to 9 young to a litter. By 1938, however, Robert Atkinson lamented that the unique St Kilda house mice 'really were gone . . . It seemed a sad little story, tacked on to the human saga of St Kilda; common house mice had come in with man so long ago that their generations had gradually formed a new race; now the men had gone and their small camp followers were to be written off as extinct.'

Field mice *(Apodemus sylvaticus hirtensis)* live only on Hirta and Dùn, reaching as far as the summit of Conachair. After the house mice became extinct, the field mice extended their range and moved into the houses. They also became more numerous and more active by day. Interestingly, there is no known case of field mice co-existing with house mice in the absence of humans. So if there had been no field mice on St Kilda in the first place it seems that the house mice might have survived, even in the absence of humans. Looking back, it is perhaps a pity that no St Kilda house mice were transferred to Boreray or Soay, where mice had never previously established.

Compared with the short 'hair' of the house mouse, the St Kilda field mouse has long, soft and fluffy fur, rather like

St Kilda National Nature Reserve St Kilda mice

a vole. The throat, chest and belly are white, the hind foot broad and more robust than that of mainland mice, although the 10cm tail seems somewhat delicate, and breaks easily. Males can weigh up to 55g, with a head and body length up to 13cm.

St Kilda mice are so much larger and heavier than their Scottish mainland counterparts that they might be mistaken for a young rat. This once happened to an expert who should have known better! As one might expect, this caused a mild panic since rats would cause havoc to the wrens, mice and of course the seabirds. Fortunately though, rats have not yet reached St Kilda and that possibility must be guarded against at all costs. The threat of mink or any other carnivore stowing away on boats is also very real, and it is an all too common disaster on many other offshore islands around the world.

▲ Village Street

Viking mice

It has long been recognised that island field mice were distinct from those on the British mainland and in 1940 no less than 15 separate sub-species were being proposed. Nowadays, only the field mice from Rum, the largest of the island forms, retains its subspecific status. One study has highlighted how all these island mice were more akin to those from Norway than to British mainland populations. The Vikings were proposed as the most likely agent of dispersal, especially since the St Kildan and Icelandic mice were the most Norwegian of all. Mice could easily stow away in the belongings, foodstuffs and animal fodder carried by sea-faring colonists, but whether the Vikings or some more recent immigrants were responsible remains a matter of debate.

Caoraich Shòdhaigh

Soay sheep

POPULATION UPS AND DOWNS SLUAGH AG ATHARRACHADH

▲ Soay sheep

It is often a feature of remote islands that they preserve primitive forms of plants and animals that have never been exposed to competition from later, more successful types. St Kilda is no exception, having its own sheep breeds. It is a tribute to the St Kildans that they managed to persist with one primitive breed – the Soay – that is, after all, better adapted to the rigorous conditions of the islands but not necessarily the easiest to handle. It seems that these Bronze Age relics might have been 'hunted' instead of shepherded, since they scatter rather than let themselves be rounded up by dogs or men.

▲ Dark Soay rams in summer

Latterly, the islanders adopted a Blackface breed on both Hirta and Boreray, so the old sheep survived only on Soay, from where they get their name. When the inhabitants finally abandoned St Kilda in 1930 they removed all sheep from Hirta. However, two years later the islands' owner, the Marquis of Bute, had 107 Soay sheep – 20 tups, 44 ewes, 22 ram lambs and 21 ewe lambs – transferred from Soay to Hirta. Despite this limited gene pool, the Soay flock on Hirta are known today to have a surprisingly high degree of genetic variation. Three quarters of the sheep have a brown coat and the rest are light fawn. About 5% have white markings on the face or body. The rams and about half the ewes carry horns.

10-12% of the males and 65% of the females have small and crumpled horns. These rams are poorly

equipped for fighting and do not perform well in the rut. However, they do tend to live longer and so

have more opportunities to participate. Adult male Soay sheep reach 36kg or more in summer and adult females about 25kg.

By 1939 there were about 500 sheep on Hirta and the first organised census in 1952 revealed 1114. The presence of this second Soay flock on Hirta has helped ensure the future of the breed. Also, since the island of Soay was so difficult to access, the Hirta flock – especially those in Village Glen – were chosen for a unique long term study, first by the Nature Conservancy and latterly by various university groups. They have been counted annually since 1955 and average 1200 animals (ranging from 600 to 1968). Hirta therefore

supports a density of some 0.9 ewes per hectare – a relatively low figure, as the equivalent for mainland sheep is about 2.5.

The counts reveal periods of rapid increase to a high density, followed by periodic crashes when up to 60% of the population can die in a single winter. 1996 was one of the highest counts ever but the population declined little the following winter, indicating that high density does not necessarily trigger a crash. Crashes have also occurred from relatively low populations when the sheep might have been expected to be in good condition. Gales in March seem to be involved but the number of deaths overwinter seems to be made worse by parasites, particularly gut worms.

Parasite loads increase as the density of sheep increases and indeed, Soay sheep demonstrate one of the highest resistances to parasites of any breed. Although they share the same parasites as Blackfaces, they seem to be more effective in dealing with them, which has important implications for commercial sheep farming.

The rut takes place in November, with each ewe sexually active for one or two days only. Inevitably, there is strong competition amongst the rams and as they do not have much time to feed during this intense mating activity, large numbers die over the winter. This means there are more ewes in the population, varying annually from three to eight for every ram.

Lambs are born after a pregnancy of 151 days. This is several days longer than modern breeds, which also mature faster. Most births are clumped within 10 days on either side of 20 April, and proceed with fewer problems than other breeds. A small number of twins are born (and at least one instance of triplets) but the survival in these multiple births is poor. Lambs weigh about 2kg at birth and are feeding independently by July. The ewes can then spend the rest of the summer regaining condition before the rut in November.

Those animals that survive population crashes can enjoy a ripe old age – the oldest tagged ewe was 15 when she died. For a ram to live to 10 is rare, however, and most die before they reach six. The long term study of individually-marked sheep has allowed their life-time reproductive success to be documented. This remarkable story is backed up with DNA analysis, feeding habits, energy use, parasite cycles and weather recording.

▲   Tan-coloured Soay ewe with lamb

Caoraich Bhoraraigh

Boreray sheep

THE SKILLED CLIMBERS   NA STREAPADAIREAN EALANTA

Towards the end of the 19th century the St Kildans kept Blackface sheep both on Hirta and on Boreray. They took all the Hirta sheep off when they left in 1930 but abandoned those on Boreray to their fate. This steep crag lies some 6 km to the northeast and is difficult to access at the best of times. With dark collars and white or tan markings, Boreray sheep look like a cross between Soays and Blackface. In fact they are survivors of a cross between early Blackfaces and the old Scottish Shortwool sheep that still survive on North Ronaldsay in Orkney and in the Shetland Islands.

© Keith Brockie 2002

▲ Boreray

Borerays have large curving horns, especially on the rams, and usually have creamy-brown fleeces. About a quarter of them are grey-brown, a few blackish and the occasional one tan in colour. The face varies from black and white to greyish, with a few completely black, tan or white. Both Soay and Boreray lambs withstand cold and wet better than commercial sheep, but freely make use of shelter in the cleits. They are also skilled climbers, so the varied landforms of the island cliffs offer shelter too. Lambs bond quicker with their mothers than mainland sheep and are quicker to suck, all of which helps them to survive in such exposed conditions. Lambing percentages on Boreray can be high and are equivalent to shepherded flocks in the Scottish Borders.

The sheep on Boreray fluctuate from 350 or so to nearly 700, probably influenced by the weather. Indeed, it has become obvious recently that

Boreray sheep cycle in unison with the Soays on Hirta and probably also with those on Soay itself. Only about 60 out of Boreray's 77 rocky hectares can act as pasture for the sheep so the density of animals is high at about 12 per hectare. This is five times the density of hill sheep in the Hebrides and lowland sheep only reach densities of 15 per hectare. Although the vegetation on Boreray is soaked in salt spray, it is well manured by guano from the nesting seabirds. The variety of plants in this well-grazed grassland has a thick and widespread root system. This helps, along with compaction of the soil by the sheep flock, to reduce erosion. The survival of such a high density of sheep on such steep, windswept slopes does not appear to be a problem.

From time to time, following a crash, visitors come across many sheep carcasses scattered over Hirta. This sometimes reopens the debate as to whether St Kilda's sheep should be left unmanaged. However, it is important to remember that the original sheep population on Soay never had much management, possibly for hundreds or even thousands of years. Given the remoteness of both Soay and Boreray, it would be almost impossible to maintain any form of management there anyway.

Loss adjusters

Dr Morton Boyd, who began the sheep study in the 1950s, later concluded that to lose the sheep altogether would not only remove assets of great cultural, historical and scientific interest but also 'reduce the diversity of plant life which their grazing sustains on the islands. . . The sheep are now adjusted over centuries to meet the rigours of their world.'

◀ Boreray ram

Ròin, muic-mhara, leumadairean agus pèileagan
Seals, whales, dolphins and porpoises

NEW FAMILIES IN VILLAGE BAY   TEAGHLAICHEAN ÙRA ANNS A' BHÀIGH

Only Atlantic grey seals visit the shores of St Kilda. The St Kildans once hunted them, the dried skins going towards rent payments. Up to a hundred pups are born in October and November, but few places on the exposed, steep rocky coastline prove as suitable as the flat, sloping slabs of Dùn in Village Bay. After the people left, and before the Army built their camp, some pups were born on the beach below the Manse. Around 300 to 400 adults and juveniles spend time on the shores throughout the year, with the main concentrations in Glen Bay, Soay Sound and around the Cambir.

Grey seal and pup ▶

Sightings of these sea mammals have increased in recent years, particularly in the summer months May to August. This is probably due to better and more accurate recording. Ten species have been sighted from St Kilda so far, all but one of them known to occur regularly off the Scottish west coast in summer. The exception was a rare Sowerby's beaked whale, which washed up in Village Bay on 29 September, 1994.

Minke whales are the most common, mostly in ones or twos. Killer whales are the next most frequent. Pods vary in size, with an estimated 40 to 50 animals seen in July 1984. Not surprisingly, Risso's dolphin is also commonly identified as it is the largest and most distinctive of the smaller dolphins. Farther out to sea, occasional groups of white-sided and white-beaked dolphins are seen. Porpoises were first reported in 1988, but as with the occasional bottle-nosed or common dolphins, usually involve only single animals.

▲ Minke whale

Other **animals**

Amphibians rarely manage to raft out to any offshore island as they lack waterproof skin. Nor have any reptiles managed to establish on St Kilda. However, there have been seven recent records of leathery turtles in the waters around the islands, all from late July through to September. There have been 20 sightings of basking sharks since 1986, with up to three individuals at one time. A few might be spotted in May and June but most during July and August. There is also a record of a sunfish in June 1998 and five more during June and July 2000.

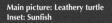

Main picture: Leathery turtle
Inset: Sunfish

And finally

SNH teams have intensely surveyed the underwater world around St Kilda and this deserves more attention than this booklet can give. The purpose here has been to focus on the land, how the landforms came about and how the islands came to be inhabited by a variety of plants and animals. We also set out to explain why, at the end of the day, its variety of life forms is so limited compared with the rest of Scotland.

Nevertheless, St Kilda is home to a fascinating range and quantity of plants and animals, some of which the islands themselves have modified to suit the extreme environment. The St Kilda archipelago is probably one of the best demonstrations in the whole of the British Isles of how islands can influence their inhabitants. In this respect it may not be quite as dramatic as the Galapagos Islands or New Zealand, but it is unique in its own right and well worthy of the various conservation titles it has attracted over the years.

The National Trust
for Scotland

The National Trust for Scotland
Balnain House
Huntly Street
Inverness
IV3 5HR

Tel: 01463 232034

Scotland's natural heritage is a local, national and global asset.
SNH promotes its care and improvement, its responsible
enjoyment, its greater understanding and appreciation, and its
sustainable use, now and for future generations.

Scottish Natural Heritage
Stilligarry
South Uist
HS8 5RS

Tha dualchas nàdair Alba cudthromach aig ìre ionadail, nàiseanta
agus air feadh an t-saoghail. Tha SNH a' cur air adhart a bhith ga
leasachadh agus a' toirt an aire air, ach am faigh daoine toileachas
às le bhith faiceallach. Tha SNH airson gum bi daoine a' tuigsinn
mun àite agus a' cur luach air agus ag obrachadh an fhearainn
ann an dòigh a tha taiceil ach am mair e san àm ri teachd.

Dualchas Nàdair na h-Alba
Stadhlaigearraidh
Uibhist a Deas
HS8 5RS

Photography by Aberdeen University, Steve Austin, Laurie Campbell,
David Donnan/SNH, Lorne Gill/SNH, Chris Gomersall, Mike
Lane/NHPA, Roy Leverton, John Love/SNH, Pete Moore/SNH, Doug
Perrine/Planet Earth Pictures, Keith Ringland, Glyn Satterley, Sue Scott,
James Smith, Masa Ushioda/imagequestmarine.com, Jim Vaughan,
David Whitaker.

Drawings by Keith Brockie, John Love/SNH, Natural History Museum.

Map by Wendy Price

Text by John Love

Gaelic translations by Màiri Gillies

Design by Exodus[AD], Kinross

Printed by Nevisprint NP2.5K1004 *on environmentally friendly pap*

SNH Publications

Battleby, Redgorton, Perth, PH1 3EW

Tel: 01738 444177

Fax: 01738 458613

E-mail: pubs@snh.gov.uk

Website: www.snh.org.uk

English website www.kilda.org.uk
Gaelic website www.hiort.org.uk

ISBN 1 85397 403 X

Price £4.95

ISBN 1-853974-03-X

9 781853 974038 >